Good For Me
Milk and Cheese

Sally Hewitt

PowerKiDS press.

New York

Notes for Teachers and Parents

Good for Me is a series of books that looks at ways of helping children to develop a positive approach to eating. You can use the books to help children make healthy choices about what they eat and drink as an important part of a healthy lifestyle.

Look for milk and cheese when you go shopping.
- Look at the different types of milk and cheese in your local supermarket.
- Read the ingredients on packages to see if the food contains milk and cheese.
- Buy something new. Have fun preparing it and eating it with children.

Talk about different food groups and how we need to eat a variety of foods from each group every day.
- Milk and cheese are packed with vitamins, minerals, and protein.
- Talk about the ways vitamins and minerals help to keep us strong and healthy.

Talk about how we feel when we are healthy, and the things we can do to help us to stay healthy.
- Eat food that is good for us.
- Drink plenty of water.
- Enjoy fresh air and exercise.
- Sleep well.

Published in 2008 by The Rosen Publishing Group, Inc.
29 East 21st Street, New York, NY 10010

First Edition

Produced by Tall Tree Ltd.
Editor: Jon Richards
Designer: Ben Ruocco
Consultant: Sally Peters

Library of Congress Cataloging-in-Publication Data

Hewitt, Sally, 1949—
  Milk and cheese / Sally Hewitt. — 1st ed.
    p. cm. — (Good for me)
  Includes index.
  ISBN 978-1-4042-4268-5 (lib. bdg.)
  1. Dairy processing—Juvenile literature. 2. Cheesemaking—Juvenile literature. 3. Milk—Juvenile literature. 4. Cheese—Juvenile literature. I. Title.
  SF250.5.H49 2008
  641.3'7—dc22
                          2007032592

Manufactured in China

Picture credits:
Cover top Alamy/Photo Network, bottom Dreamstime.com/Edyta Pawlowska, 1 and 9 Alamy/Huw Jones, 4 Dreamstime.com/Jay Schulz, 5 Dreamstime.com/Olga Lyubkina, 6 Dreamstime.com/Jan De Wild, 7 Dreamstime.com/Anneke Schram, 8 Alamy/Agripicture Images, 10 Dreamstime.com/Edyta Linek, 11 Dreamstime.com/Carole Gomez, 12 Corbis/Phil Schermeister, 13 Dreamstime.com/Gordana Sermek, 14 Corbis/A. Inden/zefa, 15 Dreamstime.com/Monika Adamczyk, 16 Rex Features/Phanie Agency, 17 Corbis, 18 Dreamstime.com/Masha Telepneva, 19 Dreamstime.com/Galina Barskaya, 20 middle Dreamstime.com/Christine Mercer, bottom left Dreamstime.com/Sarah Louise Johnson, bottom middle Dreamstime.com/Edyta Pawlowska, bottom right Dreamstime.com, 21 top middle Dreamstime.com/Edyta Pawlowska, center left Dreamstime.com/Steve Lovegrove, upper center Alamy/Ingram Publishing, center right Dreamstime.com/Heath Doman, center Dreamstime.com/Jack Schiffer, bottom left Dreamstime.com/Rena Schild, bottom middle Dreamstime.com/Joe Gough, bottom right Dreamstime.com/Elena Elisseeva, 23 Alamy/Photo Network

Contents

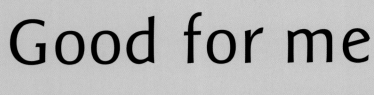

Good for me

Everyone needs to eat food and drink water to live, grow, and be **healthy**. All the food we eat comes from animals and plants. Milk and cheese are food from animals.

Most of the milk we drink comes from cows. Sheep and goats give us milk, too.

Milk, cheese, cream, and yogurt are all known as dairy foods.

Cheese, cream, yogurt, and butter are all made from milk. Milk and cheese are delicious to drink and eat. They are good for you!

Protein

Milk and cheese are a kind of food called **protein**. Protein helps you to grow and gives you energy. Milk and cheese are also full of **vitamins** and **minerals** that give you healthy eyes, skin, and hair.

Baby calves drink milk from their mothers, because they need protein to grow.

Milk and cheese contain vitamin D and the mineral calcium. These help you to grow strong bones and teeth.

You can have three portions of dairy food every day, such as a piece of cheese or a glass of milk.

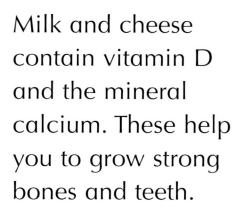

Lunchbox

Pack a carton of fresh milk for your lunchtime drink.

7

Milk

On the farm, cows are **milked** every morning and evening. The fresh milk is kept cold. A tanker collects the milk and takes it to a **dairy**.

A machine takes milk from the cows' **udders**.

Machines at a dairy fill thousands of bottles and cartons with milk every day.

At the dairy, the milk is heated to kill any **germs**. Then the milk is put into bottles and cartons and taken to stores.

Lunchbox

Ask an adult to mix a banana with some milk in a blender to make a tasty smoothie.

Cream and butter

When milk is left to stand, the thick part of the milk rises to the top. This is the cream. Cream contains a lot of fat.

Some kinds of cream are runny and can be poured onto food. Beating air into cream makes it thicker.

Butter is made by stirring or shaking cream until it becomes thick and yellow.

Butter is used for cooking and spreading on bread.

Lunchbox

Try using **Greek yogurt** on peach cobbler instead of whipped cream for a healthier option.

Cheese

Cheese is made by warming up milk. A substance called **rennet** is added to turn the warm milk into thick **curd**. Curd is made into soft cheeses, such as cream cheese, cottage cheese, and ricotta.

As the curd forms, it leaves behind a watery liquid called **whey**.

Hard cheese takes longer to make. The curd is squeezed and left to dry. Some cheeses, such as blue cheese, contain **mold**, which adds blue specks to them and gives them a strong flavour.

This girl is eating a piece of cheddar, which is a kind of hard cheese.

Lunchbox

Try different hard and soft cheeses in your lunchbox.

13

Yogurt

Yogurt is made from milk and friendly **bacteria** that are good for us. To make yogurt, milk is heated up and the bacteria are added. The milk is cooled down slowly.

As the milk cools, it sets to form thick yogurt, which can be flavored with fruit or honey.

Yogurt mixed with milk
and fruit makes a healthy
fruit smoothie.

Yogurt is sometimes stirred
into stews and soups. Yogurt
with mint, cucumber, lemon
juice, and garlic makes a dip
called tzatziki.

Lunchbox

Make a sandwich with
pita bread, falafels, and
homemade tzatziki.

Buying and storing

Milk, soft cheese, cream, and yogurt need to be kept cold to stay fresh. Stores and supermarkets keep them inside large chiller cabinets to keep them fresh.

Dairy products are printed with a sell-by date, so you can check if they are still good to eat or drink.

Milk will stay fresh
in a fridge for
about a week.

Dairy foods soon start to turn
bad if they are left in a warm
place. Put them in the fridge as
soon as you can.

Lunchbox

A thermos keeps things
cold. Put milk in
a thermos to keep it
cold until lunchtime.

Cooking milk and cheese

Milk is used to make sauces, soups, and desserts. It can be mixed with flour and eggs to create pancake mix. This is poured into a hot pan to make pancakes.

Pancakes can be eaten with toppings such as fruit, maple syrup, and nuts.

Cooking cheese melts it and makes it soft and runny. Melted cheese can be cooked with cauliflower or pasta to make a healthy meal.

Lunchbox

Add some feta cheese or goat's cheese to a salad for your lunchbox.

Pizzas are topped with melted cheese and tomato sauce.

Food chart

Here are some examples of foods and drinks that can be made using three types of dairy foods. Have you tried any of these?

Milk

Bowl of cereal

Milkshake

Custard

Cheese

Pizza

Baked potato
with cheese

Lasagne

Butter

Birthday cake

Garlic bread

Pancakes

A balanced diet

This chart shows you how much you can eat of each food group. The larger the area on the chart, the more of that food group you can eat. For example, you can eat a lot of fruit and vegetables, but only a little oil and sweets. Drink plenty of water every day, too.

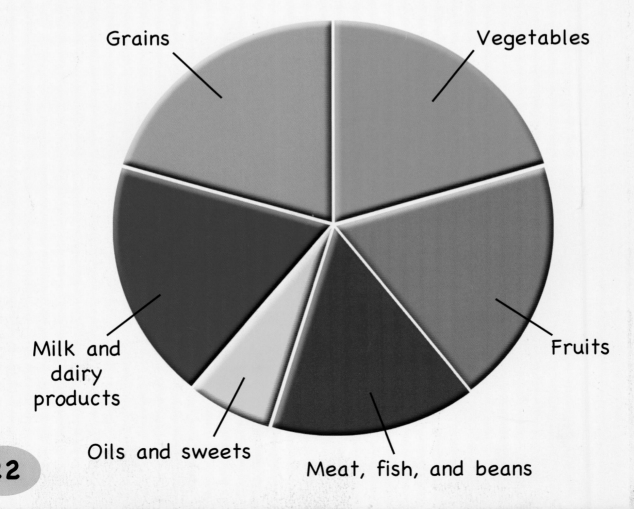

Grains

Vegetables

Milk and dairy products

Fruits

Oils and sweets

Meat, fish, and beans

Our bodies also need exercise to stay healthy. You should spend at least 20 minutes exercising every day, so that your body stays fit and healthy.

Swimming is a great form of exercise that uses muscles all over your body.

23

Glossary

Bacteria Tiny creatures that can be good for you.

Curd A thick substance formed when rennet is added to milk.

Dairy A building where milk is bottled.

Germs Tiny creatures that can be harmful and can make you sick.

Greek yogurt A type of thick yogurt with a slightly sour taste.

Healthy When you are fit and not sick.

Minerals Important substances in food. Calcium is a mineral that helps to build strong bones.

Mold A fungus that is found in some cheeses.

Protein A type of food that helps you to grow.

Rennet A substance that is added to milk to turn it into cheese.

Vitamins Substances that help our bodies stay healthy.

Whey A watery liquid left behind when rennet is added to milk.

Index

Web Sites
Due to the changing nature of Internet links, PowerKids Press has developed an online list of Web sites related to the subject of this book. This site is regularly updated. Please use this link to access this list: www.powerkidslinks.com/gfm/milch